QUEEN VICTORIA

A biography of the long-reigning Queen Victoria

Table of Contents

Introduction 1

Chapter One: Once Upon A Time There Was A Princess 2

Chapter Two: The Princess Becomes A Queen 5

Chapter Three: The Queen Finds Her Prince 10

Chapter Four: The Queen Becomes A Mom 23

Chapter Five: The Children Grow Up 28

Chapter Six: There Were Rumors 32

Chapter Seven: Even Queens Cannot Escape Death 36

Final Words 42

Introduction

Thank you and congratulations on choosing this book!

This book aims to serve as a biography of sorts, of the great Queen Victoria.

In the following chapters you will receive an insight into what the life of Queen Victoria was like, from her tumultuous childhood, to her eventual death at the old age of 81.

The Queen endured multiple assassination attempts, vicious rumors, the early death of her husband and also of multiple children during her more than 60 years on the throne. She ruled over ¼ of the globe and over 400-million subjects during her incredible reign.

The story of Queen Victoria is truly a fascinating one, filled with many trials and tribulations.

So, please, delve into the pages of history and learn about the interesting life of Queen Victoria! Once again, thanks for taking the time to pick up this book – I hope you find it to be both an entertaining and interesting read.

Chapter One: Once Upon A Time There Was A Princess

This princess was born as Alexandrina Victoria on May 24, 1819, in London, England. She was born to the Duchess of Kent, and her father happened to be the fourth son of George III. Victoria was the fifth in line to the throne. There was very little chance for her to ever become Queen.

Victoria had three uncles that were ahead of her in having succession to the throne, but all three of them were elderly. Victoria being only eight months old when her father died January 23, 1820, at Sidmouth at the Woolbrook Cottage, she did not even remember him. He died of pneumonia. They buried him at Windsor Castle in St. George's Chapel. He and his father died six days apart. Since her father had died before she was even eight months old, it made it suddenly much more likely that she may become Queen one day.

Victoria was raised in Kensington Palace. Her education was managed by her governess, Baroness Lehzen. The was taught arithmetic, music, drawing, and languages. She was gifted when it came to painting and drawing, and she developed a passion for journal writing. Her mother, now a widow was so lonely after the death of her father that she came to depend solely on the servant of her deceased husband who was power hungry. His name was John Conroy.

After her father, had died, her mother sheltered Victoria more than ever.

After her two uncles, had died, Victoria then became the heir to her only surviving uncle, King William IV.

Victoria's mother did very little to endear herself to of her late husband's relatives. Her mother's "advisor" Conroy had his personal aspirations. Some of that era could feel power was just within their reach and would do whatever they could to attain it. So in the fall of 1835, Conroy and the Duchess tried their level best to force Victoria, who was very sick at that point, to sign a document that would make Conroy her personal secretary and stated that she would not come of age until she was 21 instead of 18. Victoria told him in no uncertain terms that she was not going to sign.

Victoria was totally dominated by some very strict rules as a young lady. Everyone called it the 'Kensington System.' One devised by who else, but Conroy.

Victoria's uncle, William IV had some idea of what was going on. He delivered a speech on his birthday, and his wish was that he could live nine more months because he believed that the Duchess of Kent was now surrounded by evil people advising her and she was acting in an improper manner. It was embarrassing for Victoria and the Duchess.

The King's wish came true, but barely so. Victoria had only been 18 for one month when her uncle died. They woke Victoria early on the morning of his death and told her that she was now the Queen.

She had to share a room with her mother so she never had any time alone. Her father's servant designed this system, and he wanted to manipulate her in every way he could so he could gain more power and influence for himself.

When Victoria turned 13, she was given a tour of the Midlands so that Conroy could take her around and show her off to the public. Victoria hated this. It was tiresome and boring, and she became more stubborn by the day. It was at this point she started to keep a diary.

Just weeks after Victoria turned 18, her uncle William IV passed away, and Victoria found herself as queen. Her first

request/demand as queen was to have an hour to herself -
something she had not had in years.

Victoria then moved into Buckingham Palace deciding that
it would be her official home in London. She started making her
demands and enforcing them by making her mother live in
distant rooms of the Palace. The next step she took was to ban
John Conroy, her mother's courtier that had made her life so
very miserable – from any of her state rooms. The young queen
liked her first prime minister. His name was Lord Melbourne.
He was both admiring and a fatherly figure to her. And
overnight, she became the richest woman in the world.
Parliament gave her an annuity of 385,000 pounds.

Chapter Two: The Princess Becomes A Queen

There were 400,000 people that gathered in the streets of London. They just wanted to catch a little glimpse of the new Queen on the day of her Coronation. She was crowned in Westminster Abbey.

The Princess about to become a Queen wore beautiful robes of red velvet and white satin.

The ceremony lasted five hours and was a bit chaotic since the Dean of Westminster, the one who always presided over such ceremonies, was ill. The Queen's Orb was handed to Victoria at the wrong time, and the special ring was put on the wrong finger by the Archbishop of Canterbury, causing her to take an hour to get it off her finger!

When the ceremony was over, Victoria went back to her Buckingham Palace and sat down for a family banquet. Afterward, she went out on her mother's balcony to watch the fireworks.

There were many of the townspeople who felt that Victoria had victimized Lady Flora Hastings, who was her lady in waiting.

They felt that Victoria did not make wise choices in the early part of her reign because she let her emotions guide her judgments. Victoria had heard about the false pregnancy rumors against Lady Flora Hastings and believed them. She found herself in the middle of a political crisis when the Whig government had fallen, and then Lord Melbourne resigned. A Tory Politician by the name of Robert Peel agreed to work for her as prime minister but only if she would replace some of her Whig ladies-in-waiting with Tories. She told him she would not be doing as he had bid and she reappointed Lord Melbourne. Of course, this was criticized by many who thought this was unconstitutional.

As with everyone in high office, there is a risk of danger. And so, it was with Queen Victoria. There were several attempts made on her life during her reign.

<u>Constitution Hill</u> – June 1840 – there was great trouble all through the country side. The entire Ministry was not popular, and there were several things being said about the Court festivities. Occasionally, the Queen would be received by her subjects in utter silence. But there were a couple of times that there were some unpleasant and sinister shouts that could be heard.

It was about six o'clock on July 18th, and Queen Victoria was out in the carriage with Prince Albert. A man that was leaning against a railing in the Park suddenly drew a pistol and fired at Her Majesty as she was sitting in her carriage about six yards from him. The Queen happened to be looking in a different direction and did not realize for a moment what was happening. The carriage came to a stop, but the Prince told them to go on. Prince Albert grabbed her hands and asked her if she was alright and she just laughed.

Victoria and Albert both then saw the man, and now he had a pistol in each hand, immediately he fired again. Prince Albert pulled Victoria down in the carriage beside him, and the ball passed just over the top of her head. A crowd had gathered around the shooter, and they seized him. The Queen stood up in her carriage to show everyone she was fine. Then they had the driver take them rapidly back to the Palace so they would be able to let everyone know they were fine before they recieve exaggerated reports from anyone else.

<u>The Boy Jones </u> – During a period of two years, he got into Buckingham Palace four times and would conceal himself behind furniture or up inside the chimney during the day. At

night, he would go to the kitchen and eat and then find an empty bedroom and sleep. The servants were shocked when they would find sooty sheets in beds when they would be needed for some reason. He would brag about hearing a long talk between the Queen and Prince Albert while he was hiding behind the sofa. When he was caught, he was locked up for three months as a vagabond and a rogue. Once released from prison, he came right back to the Palace and started stalking the Queen of the Palace and the Parks when the Queen would be out driving. He was arrested again and this time was sent to go to sea. It is said he died a well to do man in one of the new colonies of America.

Second Attempt – May 30, 1842, the Queen and the Prince were returning home from the Chapel Royal. The Prince had noticed a man step out and show a pistol, but it did not fire correctly. A boy stopped by the Palace that afternoon and told them about seeing the same incident that no one else had seen. The Queen and Prince decided to go out the next day just like always, but both were very agitated. They were coming back from their drive when a "swarthy, little, ill-looking rascal," that the Prince recognized from the day before fired at the Queen. The shot passed by harmlessly. The police then seized the man before any more shots could be fired.

Hunchback named Bean – July 3rd, on a Sunday, the day after the sentence of Francis had been given, the Queen was returning with her Uncle Leopold from the Chapel Royal, St. James's. A hunchback by the name of Bean shot at the queen, but his pistol misfired. Though it was actually found to be loaded with bits of a tobacco pipe. He escaped capture for the time being and for about two weeks all hunchbacks that were in London were given a hard time. There were accused publicly and had to be ready with a decent alibi of where they were on that afternoon. They did eventually capture Bean and sentenced him to a term in prison.

Hamilton – The Queen went seven years before anyone made another assassination attempt. That was until May 19th, 1849, when a man standing by the railings of Green Park, fired at her while she was driving out on Constitution Hill. Prince Albert was riding out in front of her and the children. The Queen did not lose her composure; she stood up for a bit and told the driver to go on, and then talked to her children, to try and divert their attention. The man who shot at her was an Irishman, his name was Hamilton, and they arrested him and sentenced him to seven years' transportation since his pistol actually had no bullets.

Queen Victoria Assaulted – Victoria became the victim of outrage of someone else – one of the most cowardly and wanton of all the attacks she had been through. She had been to see her Uncle who was ill. Next, to the entrance of Cambridge House, there stood a tall man who was loitering as if he was waiting to get a glimpse of the Queen. When her carriage came out of the gateway and turned the corner, the man rushed at her and struck the Queen a sharp blow on her face with a small stick. Her bonnet was torn up by the blow, a bad bruise and a wound on her forehead was inflicted. The man was soon arrested and taken to the police station. He was about thirty years old, and a gentleman by education and birth, but not of sound mind. He was known for conspicuous conduct out in the Park, and his weirdness had lost him his position as an officer in the army. He was sentenced to seven years' transportation.

Arthur O'Connor – February 1872, when about to get off her carriage after a ride, a young man rushed at the Queen with a paper in one hand and holding a pistol in the other. John Brown, the Queen's attendant, grabbed the lad, who as usual, was found to be not right in the head. He was an Irish boy, seventeen, who had brooded over all the wrongs of his country, till he thought he could do some good by making the Queen read a petition he had drawn up. But the pistol he had did not have a ball in it. He was taken for mental care.

<u>Roderick Maclean</u> – The last attack that took place was in 1882 at Royal Windsor. The Queen who was out with Princess Beatrice, was getting into her carriage at Windsor station, when a man fired at her. His name was Roderick Maclean, who they arrested immediately. Roderick, had been formerly a respectable person, but had fallen into want, and was tried for high treason. He was found not guilty due to insanity. He was ordered imprisonment at Her Majesty's pleasure.

Chapter Three: The Queen Finds Her Prince

Yes, it is true, Victoria fell deeply in love with her first cousin, Prince Albert. He was the Prince of Saxe-Coburg and Gotha. When he visited Britain in 1839, she fell immediately head over heels for him.

There were no laws at that time for first cousins marrying as there are in the United States now.

Since Victoria was the head of state, it was necessary that she propose marriage to Prince Albert. The couple's wedding took place the next year.

As the date for her wedding got closer and closer in the early spring of 1840, Victoria became more nervous than ever. She became thin and pale, she couldn't sleep, nor could she eat, and she had a fever. Her entire body hurt and ached, and it seemed like she always had a cold. Just writing letters wore her out. Her physician examined her and told her she had the measles. Victoria lay in her bed one day at Kensington Palace on a rainy day; while trying not to be alarmed, doubts about her marriage started to crawl through her mind.

Had she not enjoyed being single the last two years of her life and just being an independent lady more than anything? If she married Albert, it would ruin all of that; her freedom would slip away from her forever! Victoria closed her eyes and began thinking about all the arrangements being prepared across the entire city. There were shoes being polished, gardens trimmed, cakes being baked, coats fitted, carriages being cleaned, and large casks of whiskey along with carts that had been piled high with food that had been made for the wedding feast.

Questions would not stop running through Victoria's head. What was her life going to be like after taking the marriage vows? What was worse? She dreaded the thoughts of having children. And, when she thought about a wife and husband being alone together, that seemed mysterious.

Then she began to wonder if she was good enough for Prince Albert? Would his eyes start wandering in a few years as Lord Melbourne had told her they might? Why was it that that the people thought that Albert would stick his nose in the politics when she was the Queen, the boss, the ruler, the one in charge? Victoria couldn't help but worry if he would criticize the way she governed the people or if he would try to control her. Would the yielding to her being the 'boss' be too much for Albert? At times Victoria felt like she did not deserve Albert. She was so plain looking, and he was so handsome. She knew her power was inherent, and her strength had come by habit, but her loving Albert had taught her to be humble. It had taken her a short time to learn how to be Queen, but would she ever learn how to be a wife?

Lord Melbourne's only task the days before the marriage was to keep Victoria's spirits boosted. He told her it was totally normal to feel all the things she was feeling before her wedding day. She reminded him that she had wanted to stay single all her life if he remembered correctly. The Lord told her that getting married was the 'normal' thing to do, but your role as the queen was "unnatural."

Victoria, though plain she was, wanted of course to feel pretty on her wedding day. She pointed this fact out to her Prime Minister. She told him she had been losing weight and looked stressed. He let her know that she looked 'great,' He told her about an article he had read in a Scottish paper. The reporter had said that Victoria had a firm mouth, open anxious nostrils, and large searching eyes. Lord Melbourne told Victoria this several times to try and reassure her and tell her that this was a very good representation and there couldn't be a better aspect said about her.

Victoria's case of the measles turned out to be nothing but nerves, which went away as soon as she saw Albert. When he made it to Buckingham Palace, she was right there at the front door standing impatiently. But in her journal, she said that seeing his *'dear, dear face again put me at rest about everything.'*

Albert was as sick as a dog from crossing the English Channel. He said he felt like a wax candle, but he was resolute and unruffled. The only thing that had Albert worried was a letter that Victoria had written him telling him that she simply would not agree to be away on a honeymoon for two weeks. She had said in the letter she was just too busy.

"Dear Albert, you have not at all understood the matter. You forget, my dearest Love, that I am the Queen, and that business can stop and wait for nothing. Parliament is sitting, and something occurs almost every day, for which I may be required, and it is quite impossible for me to be absent from London; therefore, two or three days is already a long time to be absent. I am never easy a moment if I am not on the spot."

Victoria was so deeply in love with Albert. But she loved being Queen and had a strong passion for her leadership duties. When Victoria fell in love with Albert, she never gave a thought to stepping down from her duties as Queen. She planned on still consulting on issues with the Prime Minister and reading the Cabinet documents. She wanted her hand in everything government. She felt she would be more effective and able to do even more with her husband at her side; never less. She realized she would need to be careful and not let him feel less of man as her husband, as it was, most his income was because he was married to a Queen, and in her opinion, the most famous woman in the world.

The archbishop asked Victoria if she wanted them to remove "obey" from her marriage vows, but she insisted that they remain. She did not feel that she should call him into subservience, she did not want to dominate him. That is what she did to the servants in her household, her millions of subjects, and her Cabinet. On the day of her wedding, she was complicated and contradictory, and this would not change throughout her entire life; publicly she vowed to obey Albert, and all the time privately she overruled all his wishes.

Victoria had wanted just a simple wedding. She wanted just a plain, simple dress and just a few guests and a small ceremony. But, being the Queen, this could not be had.

Albert was able to persuade her to have the wedding the people would be expecting of their Queen. He worked with her at trying to overcome being so shy in public and her being so uncomfortable when people looked at her. Albert talked her into inviting Lord Liverpool and the Duke of Wellington, even though she did not want any Tories at her wedding. He persuaded her that they needed to have the wedding ceremony in Chapel Royal of St. James's Palace. Victoria always thought that place was hideous and she hated it. She complained that everything was always made difficult for Queens and Kings.

There were some things though that Victoria could not be swayed on. Albert told her she should have only daughters of mothers that he considered were virtuous in her bridal party. He said that with the privileged being so hypocritical, that this type of morality was only a problem for the lower classes.

Victoria ignored what Albert said and chose her 12 bridesmaids per rank. She even included Lady Jersey's daughter, who had at one time been George IV's mistress.

Victoria also told them that Albert was going to sleep under her roof the night before the wedding. When her mother and the Prime Minister tried to object to this, she shrugged them off and told them what they had to say was "foolish nonsense." She knew that for herself she would sleep much better knowing he was nearby.

The day of the wedding, February 10, 1840, the skies were black and brooding that morning. Victoria slept sound, and she slept late for her, waking up at 8:45 a.m. When she woke up, she thought to herself that this would be the last time she would be in her bed by herself. This thought made her happy.

Victoria looked out her window and sat down to write a letter to her husband to be.

"Dearest, how are you today, and have you slept well? I have rested very well, and feel very comfortable today. What weather I believe, however, the rain will cease. Send one word when you, my most dearly beloved bridegroom, will be ready. Thy ever faithful, Victoria."

As they buttoned her into wedding dress of white satin, Victoria had to stand very still. The dress had a flounce made of lace with a five-metre train that was edged with orange blossoms. Her hands were shaking when she put on her Turkish diamond earrings and looped them all the way around her neck. She fastened a sapphire brooch that Albert had given her on her breast.

Her maids placed her white satin slippers on her feet as she held her feet out one at a time, and then tied the ribbons around her ankles. The dress itself was made to sit low on her shoulders, displaying her smooth, beautiful, ivory chest. Her hair being parted in the middle, then looped in buns low on each side of her head.

Victoria's clothes were carefully chosen to display her patriotism. Fabric for her dress came from the Spitalfields, the most historic place of the silk industry located in London. 200 lace-makers located in Devon, in her own country's southwest, had labored for months on the project. The pattern had to be destroyed after it was made so no one could ever copy it. The gloves she wore had been stitched in London and were made of kid leather of the English. Victoria commissioned a large amount of handmade Honiton lace to be used on her dress to try and revive the handmade lace industry (machine-made lace copies had been overtaking the handmade versions and hurting the trade.)

Victoria went to her mirror and just stared at her reflection. She could not believe it was her self. On her head, she wore just a simple wreath of myrtle and orange blossoms. In all her portraits of that day, she looks pale and young, going back and forth between dreamy and anxious.

Victoria had asked that no one else wear white to her wedding. Many took this request the wrong way and thought she was picking this color choice to let everyone know she was a virgin. In reality, it was the perfect color to highlight the lace that she had made for her gown; it was not a conventional color that most brides would wear. Before they had ways to bleach, white was rare and was expensive, not a symbol of purity but a symbol of wealth. Victoria had not been the first to wear it, but when she did, it became very popular. Lace-makers across England had a sudden surge of popularity in the work they did, and they were thrilled.

The Queen rode in her golden carriage, and the crowds were screaming. She kept her eyes looking down, and now and then she would look around quickly, give a quick nod and then look back down, and that was all the acknowledgment she would give.

The rain and winds had stopped, just like she had predicted. Vast numbers of people were out to wish her well. A Royal Wedding makes the subjects happy. For this wedding, London had been excited for weeks.

The controversial newspaper of that time, The Satirist, complained that *"We are going raving mad. Nothing is heard or thought of but doves and Cupids, triumphal arches and white favors, and last, but not least, variegated lamps and general illuminations."*

Souvenir marriage items were displayed proudly by the crowd waiting for just a glimpse of the bride. The police as was their duty, stood in stiff rows along the muddy road between the chapel, and the palace, pushing back those who were crowding in too much.

Burglars were taking advantage of no one being at their homes. Tree branches along the route from the chapel to the palace started collapsing under all the weight of people sitting or clinging to them.

When Victoria arrived at the Chapel, she went directly to her train-bearers, all dressed in white dresses chosen by her. She had given each of them a small brooch, turquoise, shaped like an eagle, as a symbol of strength and courage.

Albert was at the front of the church, waiting for her at the altar. He looked so dashing in his bright red uniform, tightly fitted and decorated. He wore the collar and the star of the Order of the Garter. This was the highest chivalry that could be attained in Britain. He blue eyes stayed fixed on his little bride as she came all the way down the aisle to him.

Florence Nightingale thought Albert a nice looking young man. She said that Victoria was *"perfectly composed and spoke distinctly and well but, every orange flower on her head was quivering, and she was very pale, and her eyes were red as if she had no sleep. She signed her name with no fear and was so anxious that Prince Albert should appear to advantage and she touched his elbow when he was about to do wrong, would show him where he needed to sign his name and put him right when he set the ring on the wrong finger. After the wedding was over, she cleared up and looked quite happy."*

The day after the wedding, there was only one report that Victoria wanted to correct and that was one that said she had cried. She had not cried one tear the whole day. She had been trained to be composed in any situation and did not want anyone to see their Queen as unsteady.

After the wedding ceremony, Victoria and Albert could go to Victoria's room for about half an hour before facing the crowds at the banquet. Victoria was placing a ring on Albert's finger as he told her there should not ever be secrets between them. Twenty-three years later, Victoria said in one of her journals that there never were any secrets between them. Before going back down to their guests, Victoria changed and put on another white dress. This one was edged in swansdown, and she had on a hat with a huge brim – a hat she could crawl into and hide.

The feast was a crazy frenzy; people beaming, curtsying, nodding and shaking hands. The new couple finally got away about four that afternoon. They left in simple fashion with three coaches, and people cheering and running alongside them.

The bride was so glad to finally be alone with Albert; something that made her happy her entire life with her husband.

Their journey was three hours to the Windsor Castle, and the couple was exhausted when they got there. Victoria had a headache when they arrived, but she went ahead and changed and lay on the couch thinking about what all had happened that day. Albert sat down and played the piano while Victoria rested. This was so much quieter than being in London; what a wonderful relief. She kept thinking back over the last few hours; the look Albert had on his face when he tried not to cry. The beautiful moment when Albert put the ring on her finger, and she became his wife. The ocean of faces and being jostled about by pushing people lining the routes; at the palace, the applause that was deafening, and most importantly, seeing Albert, so handsome in his uniform.

What she had liked most about the whole day was when they were in front of the archbishop, they were called only Victoria and Albert. When she thought about that moment, she knew that for the rest of her life, to Albert, she would always be his Victoria. To him she would not be a Queen or ruler, she would just be his lover and wife. Still laying on the couch, she rolled over onto her side and looked at Albert still playing the piano. He was playing one of his very own compositions. Albert stood up from the piano and walked over to her and started kissing her. By 10:20 p.m. they were in "one bed" as Victoria would later journal. She lay down by his side, on his chest, cuddled in his arms, and smiled into the darkness as he whispered to her.

When Victoria woke up the next morning, after getting very little sleep that night, all she could do was lay there and look at Albert's face. She could not believe how handsome he was. She felt thrilled and satisfied at the same time when she thought about their intimacy that her mind had not been able to imagine. She felt so lucky that Albert seemed to be an expert and a tender lover as well. Victoria's wedding night with Albert was the most blissful thing she had ever experienced. Her elation was noticeable in her diary entry:

"I NEVER, NEVER spent such an evening! MY DEAREST, DEAR Albert sat on a footstool by my side, and his excessive love and affection gave me feelings of heavenly love and happiness I never could have hoped to have felt before. He clasped me in his arms, and we kissed each other again and again! His beauty, his sweetness, and gentleness, - really how can I ever be thankful enough to have such a husband! Oh! This was the happiest day of my life!"

It was certainly a lustful enchantment. At breakfast, Victoria could not stop looking at him and felt that he was *"more beautiful than it was possible for her to say."* The next day, she was still cooing: *"Already the 2nd day since we have been married; his love and gentleness is beyond everything, and to kiss that dear soft cheek, to press my lips to his, is heavenly bliss. I feel a purer more unearthly feel than I ever did. Oh! Was there ever a woman ever so blessed as I am!"*

It was the little, gestures, that were so intimate she loved the most. Like when Albert would put her stockings on for her or when she would go in and watch him shave. He would slide into bed next to her and start kissing her everywhere; they would fall asleep in each other's arms. Lord Melbourne made a comment that she looked great coming back from her honeymoon; to which she told him that Albert's "affection and kindness" were "beyond everything."

Historians have long said that Queen Victoria had a high libido. Some even imply she was almost a sexual predator who almost devoured her exhausted, but tolerant husband.

Given how distraught women were about sex at this time in history for women – and limited access to abortion and contraception, no pain relief during childbirth – it is intriguing, but Victoria did not seem to make it a secret in the prudish Victorian era when it came to sex and intimate affairs. She was unabashed and unbridled physically when it came to enjoying her husband.

During the 19th century, it was suspected that women who had strong libidos were persistent: their female desires were to be considered dangerous and possibly explosive. It was thought that the woman's animal nature might take over their weaker will and they would go crazy and lose control. Women at that time were labeled as "nymphomaniacs" if they even dreamed, thought about, or if they had what was considered back then to be excessive sex.

If women were considered oversexed, some were made to have clitoridectomies or leeches were placed on their perineum. Others were told all sorts of things ranging from: adhering to strict vegetable diets, cold enemas, douching with borax, using hair pillows, and abstaining from brandy and meat.

For the most part, many married women saw sex as another chore on their ever-growing list, not something to be enjoyed. Ignorance seemed to surround women and their bodies now, and Victoria's delight in the pleasure of all things sexual was countercultural. Albert never recorded his views about sex. But he did admire her. While writing to his brother Ernest, he would brag about her off-praised breast.

The marriage of Victoria and Albert must be one of the most renowned love stories of that century. It was devoted, fruitful, and totally genuine. They brought in an era for the monarchy that would change its role forever. It would shift as one of direct power to one of indirect influence. It would change from aristocracy to the symbol of the middle class.

Victoria and Albert went to Scotland together for the first time. They thought it a beautiful and romantic place. The Highlands there made Albert think of his home in Germany.

They bought Balmoral located in Scotland and during 1853-1856, Albert himself supervised the construction of a new neo-Gothic castle for his family. It, today remains a private residence for the Royal Family. Victoria could promote the monarchy in Scotland by her frequent visits there. She would attend Highland Games and even wrote a bestselling book, "Highland Leaves," about her time and experiences there, and this boosted tourism for the country.

Victoria, with Albert's help, worked to create a highly visible monarchy to stop the growing republican movement that was going on in Britain.

Victoria herself became a patron of 150 different institutions, inclusive of dozens of charities. Albert worked and supported educational museums. They went on civic visits together to industrial towns and attended military reviews to show their support of the armed forces. They worked hard to stop the criticism that the Royal Family did not earn its keep.

Queen Victoria introduced the Victoria Cross to honor acts of great bravery during the Crimean War. It was awarded on merit and not on rank.

The War was fought by an alliance of countries that included Britain against Russia. People suspected the Queen was secretly supporting the Russian Tsar. She stopped those suspicions as she took an interest in nursing the wounded soldiers. She awarded the first Victoria Crosses personally to 62 men at a special ceremony in Hyde Park in 1857. It was the very first time that men and officers had been decorated together.

They did raise and restore the distinction of the monarchy. They preserved it from revolutions that tore down elite and royal families in Europe during the same period that Albert and Victoria were being treated lavishly in Britain. Albert would come for a short time to surpass his wife in influence, but not in longevity, sheer will, or stamina. While Victoria would endure, Albert would soar.

Queen Victoria's time changed everything for cats. Lucky cats! Queen Victoria as a child was always isolated, so animals and dolls were her companions. This may be the reason that Queen Victoria was such an avid lover of all animals and advocated for all animal rights. She had concerns about the treatment of domestic animals of all kinds and took steps that were important to help these animals.

- She funded prized for schools for essays about being kind to animals.
- She spoke publicly against the practice of using animals for experiments
- In 1840, she gave her official stamp to the Royal Society for the Prevention of Cruelty to animals.

Everyone knew about her love for dogs, but she owned all kinds of pets. She bought 2 Persian Blue cats that created a frenzy over that one breed. People everywhere wanted a cat that looked just like one that the Queen had. Later in her life, the Queen bought a white and black Persian that she named White Heather. This cat outlived her, and her son adopted her.

All the British folks followed what the Queen had done, and they fell in love with cats. Finding different breeds of cats soon got to be a great past time and of huge public interest. Having a cat for a pet that was lavished with affection was like a raging brushfire, and it swept the nation.

Chapter Four: The Queen Becomes A Mom

To everyone on the outside looking in, Queen Victoria and Prince Albert and their family seemed to be the perfect picture of family and total bliss. The reality of it all was surely not that.

Their marriage was for sure a love match.

Over seventeen years, they had nine children. Five girls and four boys.

Photographs and paintings of the royals projected a beautiful image of a wonderful family. A devoted, virtuous young couple with their fair-haired, obedient children surrounding them.

They were sexually infatuated with each other, but they stayed locked in a total power struggle. Albert kept taking on more of Victoria's work as Queen when all her pregnancies made her step aside. Victoria felt conflicted. She admired her husband as he was very talented and he certainly had the ability, but she resented not having her powers as the Queen.

They had awful fights, and Albert would be terrified by Victoria's temper fits. Forever in his mind was the worry she could have inherited George III's madness. When she would storm around the Palace, he would be reduced to slipping notes under her door.

Victoria was a productive mother, bearing nine children in 17 years. But, she "hated" being pregnant. While she was continuously pregnant, she felt more like a guinea pig or a rabbit than anything else and just did not feel nice.

Victoria suffered from postnatal depression. She also carried the hemophilia gene, this affected ten of her male descendants, that included her son, Leopold, and heir of the Russian Tsar Nicholas II.

When it came to giving birth to Leopold on April 22, 1853, the doctors gave Queen Victoria chloroform, and she loved it. She said it relieved her pain very much. She called it 'blessed chloroform,' and the effect had been delightful, soothing and quieting beyond measure.

Most of all she hated breastfeeding. She saw it as disgusting. And, to make it worse, she was never a doting mum – she felt it should be her duty to be "stern." She just didn't do the affection thing.

She and her oldest son, Bertie, they were terrible. From the very start, Victoria was disappointed in him.

Like all royal princes, they educated him at the Palace with a tutor. He did terrible with his lessons, and Victoria and Albert thought he was a halfwit. Victoria said she couldn't even call him handsome. He has a small and narrow head, then those huge features and no chin.

When Bertie was 19, he spent some of his time training in Ireland with the army. Nellie, a prostitute, got smuggled to his bed. When the story got back home to Albert, he was heart-broken, and he sat down and wrote Bertie a long, emotion-filled letter talking about his "fall."

Albert went to visit his son at Cambridge. The two went for a long walk in the rain. When Albert got back to Windsor, he fell ill, and within three weeks he was dead.

Albert in all actuality probably died of typhoid. There is also a theory that he died of Crohn's disease. For years after Albert's death, Victoria blamed Bertie. She could not stand him to even be around her.

Years later there have been records that reveal that Albert had been chronically ill off and on all his adult years and he suffered from gastric problems that were long-standing.

Since Victoria would not allow a post-mortem, his detailed medical records were reviewed by an infectious disease doctor and a gastroenterologist. Both physicians said that there was no way it was cancer or typhoid fever, and that the evidence pointed strongly to Crohn's disease.

A Crohn's specialist in Belgium, Phillippe van Hooten, also reviewed his medical record. Here is his written reply:

"You were able to collect from letters and diaries a lot of details concerning the health problems of the Prince. This data clearly demonstrated the presence of a chronic condition with several years of intermittent episodes of symptoms such as fatigue, abdominal cramps, inability to eat for several days, attacks of diarrhea, etc...leading eventually to the more serious situation of acute illness with rapid deterioration and death at the age of 42."

A chronic bowel disease that is inflammatory like Crohn's could explain a lot of the symptoms he had. Such as obstruction, diarrhea, his rheumatic type joint pains, and finally the bowel perforation and sepsis that lead up to his death.

In the last few weeks of his life, Albert suffered terrible pain in his muscles and could not sleep.

When he went to the military academy to have the talk with Bertie in the pouring rain, this just made things worse for his condition.

He came back home exhausted, very emotional and in horrible pain when the doctors made their diagnosis of typhoid fever.

Albert was a highly underrated man. He was a very ill man for most of his married life, as there was nothing available to treat the condition at that time even if they could have diagnosed him correctly. To think that he suffered so much and helped Victoria so much with the children and with the governing of her kingdom, he never really got the credit he was due.

Honestly, it took Albert dying to make Victoria into a real Queen. She had to pull herself up and look at her duties as Queen and get to it.

For the next 40 years, which was the remainder of her life, Victoria wore black for mourning and only appeared in public very rarely and reluctantly. To her people, she was the tiny "widow of Windsor" and seemed to be a grief-stricken, pathetic figure. Though in truth, it was very different.

The Queen also received servants from India to celebrate her Golden Jubilee. She promoted Abdul Karim, to be her 'teacher' or "Munshi."

He taught Victoria in Urdu and affairs of India and taught her to like curry. He was only 24, but the Queen was fascinated with the land of India. A country that she ruled but would never get to visit. Politicians of England and members living in the Palace were resentful of his position, but it did not matter to Victoria who honored him and gave him lands in India and had him accompany her on trips to the French Riviera.

Victoria's Golden Jubilee bolstered Britain's place as a global power. Soldiers of the British Empire marched through London. The Queen held a feast, and it was attended by fifty Kings and Princes from foreign lands, with the governing heads of colonies and dominions from overseas.

For Victoria's Diamond Jubilee, the elderly Queen managed to preside over several events even though she was limited due to her mobility.

She embraced new technology by sending a telegram for the first time thanking her people across her country. She accompanied the procession to St. Pauls' Cathedral. Parties were thrown everywhere in Australia and Britain, and everything was lit up. She also granted pardon to 19,000 prisoners in India.

Chapter Five: The Children Grow Up

Victoria may have been invisible, but she needed control - even over her children. She had a network of spies and informants who would report back with what her children were doing.

When Bertie married, he married Danish Princess Alexandra. Victoria told the doctor to let her know about every little detail about her health, and this included her menstrual cycle. Court balls were not to be scheduled at a time that would coincide with Alexandra's menstrual cycle.

Victoria's oldest daughter, Vicky, married Fritz, an heir to the throne of Prussia, at the age of 17. Vicky was the mother of Kaiser William II.

Even as far away as Germany, Vicky couldn't seem to get away from her mother's interference. Victoria wrote her almost every day. She tried to micromanage her daughter until it just about made Vicky crazy.

When Vicky announced that she was pregnant, Victoria told her that was the most horrid news she had heard, and it had upset her dreadfully.

Vicky's younger sister Alice also was married to a German prince. They got together to defy their mother, the Queen. Secretly they breastfed their babies. When the Queen found out she was furious and called both girls' cows.

Alice was the daughter that when her father, Prince Albert, was diagnosed with typhoid fever, took care of him until he died. When her mother went into such intense mourning, Alice acted as her mother's unofficial secretary for six months. While the court was still in mourning, Alice married German Prince Louis of Hesse. The ceremony was very private because they were in mourning and it seemed more like a funeral than it did a wedding. Alice's life in Darmstadt was not happy. There was family tragedy and poverty.

In November 1878, Alice's whole family fell ill with diphtheria. Alice's oldest daughter Victoria was the first one with symptoms; she started complaining of a stiff neck the evening of November 5th. The next morning came to the diagnosis of diphtheria. The disease soon spread. First Alix, then Irene, Marie, and Ernest. Then her husband came down with it.

Her daughter Marie became very ill on November 15th, and Alice rushed to her bedside. By the time, she got there, Marie had already choked to death. Alice was so distraught that she wrote to Queen Victoria that she could not describe the pain of losing her child. She said that the pain was beyond any words. Alice did not tell her other children about Marie's death for several weeks. She finally told Ernest in early December. He fell apart, taking it much worse than what she thought he would. Alice did something that she would normally NEVER do; she kissed him on the cheek. By December 14th, a Saturday, the very anniversary of her father's death, Alice fell ill with diphtheria. Her very last words from her lips were "dear Papa," and she fell unconscious at 2:30 a.m. Just after 8:30 a.m. she died.

Just being a daughter of Queen Victoria was no fun. It seemed like a constant game of musical chairs. Who was going to be her favorite this week? She was a helicopter mother, no matter how old you were.

Victoria changed her mind faster than most people change their underwear. She was bewildering and her rages were terrifying. She wasn't just the mother of her children; she was also their Queen and they had better not forget it.

She kept her baby girl, Beatrice (known as Baby) at the Palace; Beatrice was scared to death of her mother.

Victoria did not want Beatrice ever to get married. When Beatrice finally announced that she was also engaged to a German prince, and he was very handsome, Victoria did not speak to her for six months and finally agreed to the marriage only if they would live with her.

The real rebel of the family was Louise. She was feisty, attractive and flirtatious, and she refused to marry a German Prince that had been picked out for her. She wanted to marry Lord Lorne, the son of Duke of Argyll. This turned out to be a big mistake – the marriage was without children and was so unhappy for Louise, and the big rumor was that Lorne was homosexual.

Victoria didn't stop the control with her girls. She was just as tough with her boys. Her son Leopold was born with hemophilia, and she made sure he suffered. Victoria said he was such a plain looking child.

She worked her hardest making him live like an invalid. She would even wrap him in cotton wool. As a young boy, he was bullied by a servant that did nothing but look after him. He tried to tell his mother, but she refused to listen to him. She did not want him to leave home. But, he kept on, till he finally got to study at Oxford.

Prince Leopold was so stifled by his mother, by her wanting to keep him at home all the time, that his only hope of escaping her was to get married. Because he had hemophilia, it was hard to find a wife. He went through many, believe me. Heiress Daisy Maynard, Princess Frederica of Hanover, Princess Elisabeth of Hesse-Kassel, Victoria of Baden, and Princess Karoline Mathilde to name a few.

Victoria finally fixed him up with Princess Helen Friederike, and they married on April 27, 1882. In 1883, they had a daughter.

Now, being that Prince Leopold did have hemophilia, he had a lot of joint pain, and in the winter, it was always a bad time for him. His wife was pregnant, but she said for him to go on to the doctor and she would just stay home. He slipped and fell, it injured his knee, and he hit his head. He died early the next day from what appeared to be a cerebral hemorrhage. His son was born four months later, Prince Charles Edward. Leopold was the second of Queen Victoria's children to die.

Chapter Six: There Were Rumors

There were rumors that Queen Victoria had other men in her life.

There were also claims that Victoria found sexual interest with a very arrogant, uncouth, heavy drinking ghillie from the Highlands, a man by the name of John Brown. It further goes on to allege that they were married in a secret ceremony and that she had a child.

Here again, we have claimed that Victoria had some kind of hormonal imbalance, and wanted sex all the time. The type of sexual appetite that made some suggest nymphomania.

Let us think back for a moment to her husband, Prince Albert who was a somewhat feminine 18-year-old virgin when she first met him and saw him.

Already suspected of being a latent homosexual, Albert was asked why he had not sown his wild oat with the women. And he had told them that the species of the vice disgusted him.

It didn't matter, the Queen, three months older than him, had her eyes set on the fact that she was going to marry him, and proposed after four days of dating.

From their marriage night forward, Victoria was the one coming on to Albert. He was so unnerved and so appalled by the nightly sexual requirements and onslaught by the Queen, that he had taken to locking his bedroom doors and cowering behind them.

She would stand outside in the hall telling him to let her in because she was the Queen in the German tongue.

After all the years of being nothing but a breeding stud, Albert finally invented and installed a switch by his bed that activated mechanical locks on the bedroom doors so that none of their kids could come in and catch them having sex.

When Beatrice, the baby was born, the Queen's doctor told her that she did not need to get pregnant again. This was a dire warning. Victoria was 38 at the time. She felt her sex life with Albert was heavenly. She threw a little fit at the doctor and wailed that it meant she was not going to have any more fun in the bed.

Then four years later, Albert died of typhoid fever at 42 years old. At that time, he was no longer an attractive, slim figure of his youth, but a bald, fat, and prematurely middle-aged man.

To combat Victoria's worsening depression, John Brown was brought in from his post as Albert's ghillie down at Balmoral to be Victoria's personal groom. Immediately upon arrival he started bullying the Queen and acted as if he had always known her. This astonished everyone. Victoria's daughters called him "Momma's lover."

He even got her to drink whiskey when he drank. They preferred Begg's Best. She started calling him a "fascinating Johnny Brown." And the shocked Foreign Secretary had recorded that they slept in rooms that were adjoining, contrary to what was considered decent.

Then there was anti-Brown propaganda that claimed he was the Queen's husband but had no claim to any title. These pamphlets were being given out everywhere by Scottish socialist republican nationalist Alexander Robertson.

This story of this entire mess all showed up in 19th-century diaries of the Liberal politician Lewis Harcourt. He had claimed that the Queens chaplain, Reverend Norman Macleod, had made his deathbed confession that he had married Queen Elizabeth to John Brown.

But we will put this to hearsay for right now. Harcourt was nine years old at the time of Macleod's death, unless someone else was present at Macleod's death to pass the confession on down.

Queen Victoria started addressing Brown as 'Darling" in all her letters she wrote to him, and she also wrote the word 'Hochmagandy" – which is the old Scottish word for intercourse – and that it had happened.

There was a medical examination of the Queen after her death that brought forth light on some new findings. First and foremost, she had a ventral hernia that had damaged the walls of her abdomen, a uterus that was prolapsed, and this would have made having children impossible.

We must remember though; this was AFTER her death, not at the time she was involved with John Brown. A lot could have happened in all the years in-between.

The Press now called Victoria 'Mrs. Brown", and later, with her elevation as the Empress of India she was called 'Empress Brown.'

Brown's action in stopping an assassination attempt on Victoria's life in 1872 changed the public's mind, and made him a hero nationally and restored the Queen to popularity.

Brown died in 1883 from a horrible form of erysipelas, at the age of 56. Victoria showed her sexual appetite had not slowed down.

In 1887, she replaced Brown with a young Indian man of low-caste who was uneducated; Abdul Karim who she called her 'Munshi.'

He rose rapidly in the Palace from waiting on her table to becoming her secretary.

She gave him three houses: a bungalow on the Isle of Wight, a cottage at Windsor, and a lovely house at Balmoral, all of which he filled up with his relatives who did not have a dime to their names and were being kept on the British tax payer's dime.

In the Royal Archives in Windsor Castle, there is a Certificate of Marriage between John Brown and Queen Victoria.

Queen Victoria's great-grandson who was a painter had been confronted in New York at one of his post-war painting exhibitions by an elderly woman who told him that she thought they were related. She went on to tell him that her name was Jean Brown and she was a daughter of John Brown and Queen Victoria.

The story was that she had been shipped to America at a very early age and kept a secret for over 80 years. The lady who was entitled to a small fortune, left and was never heard from again.

There is also a story of a son born to them who died in Paris, and he was supposedly a 90- year old hermit. And then that of a second daughter, Louise Brown who also was sent to Paris per the Queens royal banker who sent her 250 pounds once a quarter. The money was to be debited in an account marked "*His Royal Highness Prince Albert Edward, Prince of Wales.*"

Chapter Seven: Even Queens Cannot Escape Death

In January of 1990, the Queen was in her room writing in her journal. She was 80 years old. She asked the good Lord that he may spare her yet a short while to be with her children, her friends, and her country.....

Then in January of 1991, she was not doing well. She wrote in her journal that she was not feeling well, and that she felt weak.

January 14, 1901: Dr. James Reid was the Queen's personal doctor, and he kept extensive notes on the queen's health. The Queen trusted him, and he was a valued member of the Royal household. In his notes, he stated that he felt that the Queen's mind was shutting down. He had noticed that she was finding it hard to concentrate and when she would wake up she had trouble figuring out where she was and who the maids, the ones with her every day, were.

January 16, 1901: For the first time in his life and service to the Queen he examined her in her bed. It was forbidden and against all etiquette. The maids were worried because they couldn't get her to wake up. She just would not come all the way awake.

The doctor told her private secretary, Ponsonby of how ill the Queen was and that she should not see anyone. She was very ill and should have no visitors. Ponsonby would have none of it. But he finally agreed although be it begrudgingly.

Late that evening, before the Queen was even awake enough to be placed in her wheelchair; she was confused, her speech was slurred, and labored. Another doctor was called in for a second opinion, and he said the Queen was just fine. He said that the Queen had talked to him about all kinds of things with vigor and interest and was quite herself.

The doctors argued. Reid felt the Prince of Wales needed to be notified.

Within ten minutes of the consulting doctor leaving, the maids called Reid back up to see the Queen. Victoria was again confused and exhausted. Reid was not only angry; he was concerned that he had made efforts to notify the correct people and they had been ignored. So, he decided to notify the Prince of Wales himself.

January 17, 1901: Reid became more worried. Her face was drawn on one side, and she was more confused and drowsy than the day before. He was sure she had had a stroke. He realized the enormity of the situation, and it was his duty to notify someone about her condition. She could not last much longer.

A circular went out, but it was all a big lie about her condition. To avoid the public being upset, the circular was 'selectively edited.'

January 19, 1901: Her children who were there acted like their mother was just fine. The doctor could not believe they were acting so foolishly and were so blind. He ordered that the Prince of Wales be phoned immediately and told he needed to stay in London and not go on holiday, but be prepared to go to the Isle of Wight as soon as possible. A train was prepared and sitting at Victoria Station for the Prince and his sister, Louise.

Two hours later, everyone was in a dither. Amidst the anxiety of the end of the Queen's life, there was so much that had to be done. Press had to be kept up to date and arrangements had to be made for a funeral. All kinds of royalty were coming in from all over the country, and they had to be making sleeping arrangements and preparing food for everyone.

January 20, 1901: the entire nation knew what was happening and was waiting on pins and needles. On the tiny Isle of Wight, the Queen was dying surrounded by her family. In London, people by the thousands were turned out to St. Paul's Cathedral where they went to pray.

The Queen continued her slow descent and awoke the following morning extremely restless and confused. Her breathing was much more difficult, so they gave her oxygen to see if it would help. She was helpless as she lay there. She could not even move. That evening the Queen's family stayed at her bedside. She lay in her bed barely able to speak, barely breathing, having difficulty just swallowing, barely able to recognize her children, and barely conscious.

At midnight, Bishop of Winchester was awakened and instructed to hasten to Osbourne immediately. Be prepared to stay. The Bishop knew what this meant.

January 22, 1901: The Queen could no longer swallow, and her lungs were filling with fluid. She could barely cough, and when she did breathe, her windpipe would rattle. The Bishop came in and said prayers for the Queen with the family at her side. The Prince of Wales hovered near. The Queens last word was "Bertie. She whispered this, and it brought her son who was 60 years old and lived in fear of her all his life to bury his face and cry.

As odd as it may seem, it was the Kaiser that was finally admitted into his Grandmother's bedroom that helped the Queen's doctor in supporting her head on a pillow. They did this for over two hours; he could not change arms as his other arm was withered and no good. It was in the crook of her grandson's arms she died.

At 6:25 p.m. the Bishop was brought back in quickly, as he started to pray, Victoria looked at the Prince of Wales, but she did not appear to see them.

Reid was trying to feel for a pulse, and the Bishop administered the last rites. The Queen drew her last breath at 6:30 p.m.

There was a huge outpouring of mourners. All the adults were dressed in black, banners of purple and black were being hung from public areas and shop windows, and everything was getting a fresh coat of black paint.

All eyes turned to plans for the funeral of their Queen.

February 1, 1901: Queen Victoria's coffin left Osbourne to be taken to the Royal yacht, The Alberta, where it then sailed to Portsmouth. The sounds of gunfire could be heard from the warships. The Prince of Wales –King Edward VII (Bertie) now 61 years old – followed behind. From this point, the coffin would go by train to London – arriving to immense crowds at the station. The coffin was then carried by a gun carriage that was decorated. Upon it was the Imperial Crown, scepter, a collar of the Order of the Garter, and the orb – which all made the procession through the streets lined with soldiers. Behind the coffin was the New King Edward VII as well as a large list of dignitaries that had come from all over the world. There was Kaiser Wilhelm II, King Carlos of Portugal, Archduke Franz Ferdinand, King George I of the Hellenes, King Leopold II of the Belgians just to name a few. The estimate was over a million folks from all backgrounds and classes had come to London to say goodbye to the Queen.

Princess Maud made note that even though there were so many people in London, you could not hear a sound when the coffin passed by them. The coffin would travel from London to Windsor on the Royal train.

February 4, 1901: crowds again gathered in Windsor and cried as they watched the Queen's coffin be carried from the train to Windsor Castle, where she would lay in state in the Albert Memorial Chapel.

From there, the Queen would be taken by her family to their mausoleum where she would be laid to rest next to Albert who had died 40 years earlier.

After a moving service and a Blessing in the Mausoleum, the Royal family passed one by one over the platform looking at the grave containing the coffins of their mother and father side by side. The new King knelt by the grave with his young son and wife, in silence for a few minutes, before they walked on.

A beautiful stone figure had been sculpted of the Queen by Baron Marochetti, who had also sculpted one of Prince Albert which had lay on his grave ever since he had died. The one of the Queen had been kept stored for 40 years, waiting for her death. The figure of Victoria when placed on the tomb was such that she was looking at Prince Albert, the love of her life, with whom after forty long years, was finally again reunited.

Since the old Queen believed in long mourning periods. The public was gearing up for a long period of wearing black to honor Victoria. King Edward VII limited the time of mourning so that the people could cease in three months.

King Edward VII had his coronation in August 1902 and only lived until 1910.

Edward smoked all the time, up to twenty cigarettes and then twelve cigars all in one day. In 1907 he developed a type of cancer that showed up affecting skin that was next to his nose. It was cured with radium. Getting towards the end of his day his bronchitis bothered him worse and worse. He suffered a loss of consciousness even though momentarily during a visit to Berlin in February 1909. In March 1910, while he was staying at Biarritz, he collapsed. He decided to stay there to recuperate. On April 27, he came back to Buckingham Palace, still not over the bronchitis. Alexandra, his wife, got back from visiting her brother.

The next day, the King had several heart attacks. He would not go to bed. He said he was going not to give in and that he was going to work until the very end. When he would have a moment of lucidness, his son, Prince of Wales told him that his horse, Witch of the Air, won at Kempton Park that day. The King said he was glad about that. At 11:30 p.m. he lost total consciousness for what would be the last time, and he passed away within 15 minutes.

Alexandra did not want his body moved. She made them leave it there for eight days after he had died. She let visitors into his room. Finally, on May 11, the late King, dressed in uniform was placed in a beautiful oak coffin. It was moved on May 14 to the throne room, where they sealed it and it, lay in state, while four guards stood at each corner. Despite the amount of time since his death, Alexandra said that his body was still 'wonderfully preserved.' On May 17, a coffin was placed on a gun carriage, pulled by the black horse to Westminster Hall, with the new King and his family behind the coffin. After a brief service, the family left, the hall was opened for the public, and over 400,000 filed past his coffin for two days.

Victoria had ruled over a huge Empire which included over 400-million subjects, and lands that covered more than ¼ of the globe. But, she would never forget the men she had leaned on for support. At her request, in her coffin was placed a plaster cast of Albert's hand and one of his dressing gowns. And unbeknownst to everyone but the funeral director, she had a picture of John Brown's hair and a picture of him placed in her hand and gold wedding band from John. She requested that Abdul Karim be one of the main mourners at her funeral. She was a true ruler, getting her way even into death.

Final Words

Queen Victoria led an interesting life. As a child, it seems she never felt loved by anyone. Her mother tried to find ways around family tradition so that she could be Queen and not her daughter. She confined her daughter and did not allow her to have any friends or companionship.

It was not until she met the love of her life, Prince Albert, that she ever felt truly happy.

From that moment on, she had an incredible impact over the world, ruling over more than ¼ of the globe, for over 60 years.

Queen Victoria lived an incredible life that can be quite hard to fathom. Hopefully this book has given you some insight into what an incredibly fascinating existence she had.

Thank you once again for taking the time to read this book – I hope you enjoyed it! Please, take the time to leave a review on Amazon, it helps me to continue producing these books. Also, don't forget to take a look at the other biographical books I have available on Amazon.

Thanks for reading!